*Acid and Tender* is rich with music, vivid detail and the tensions suggested in the title. The poems that explore Frida Kahlo's life and art mirror her surreal imagery and passion, a worthy homage. Jen Rouse gets to the heart of both poetry and painting when she writes, *I paint/ the flowers so they/ will not die.*
—Ellen Bass, Judge of the Charlotte Mew Prize

Jen Rouse's poems are the dark and delightful imaginings of a born fairytale maker. Into the woods we go, there to find a girl with a hummingbird head, a resurrected Frida, a pair of small ruthless kings, a phoenix in a coffee shop, blow darts, knives, wings of Jurassic proportion. All is fabulous, all is makebelieve. Or not. Reader: read carefully. These poems walk the blood edge of real.
—Maureen Seaton, Author of *Fibonacci Batman: New & Selected Poems*

Jen Rouse's *Acid and Tender* embraces the tragic myth of Frida Kahlo—though not through the artist's biography. Instead, this poet approaches the iconography of Kahlo's paintings as if crafting intercessory prayers to the feminist icon. The poetry then shifts from art historical references to a personal journey that indulges the memories of being a mother, daughter, and granddaughter confronted by mythic figures. Such abstract memories, in turn, leave her readers incessantly craving more of that sweet nectar sought by the hummingbird that weaves its way through Rouse's collection.
—Christina Morris Penn-Goetsch, Professor of Art History, Cornell College

# Acid *and* Tender

# Acid *and* Tender

## Jen Rouse

HEADMISTRESS PRESS

Copyright © 2016 by Jen Rouse
All rights reserved.

ISBN-13: 78-0997914931
ISBN-10: 0997914939

This book may not be reproduced, in whole or in part, including illustrations, in any form (beyond that permitted by Sections 107 and 108 of the U.S. Copyright Law and except by reviewers for the public press), without written permission from the publishers.

Cover art © 2015 Jen Rouse
Cover & book design by Mary Meriam

PUBLISHER
Headmistress Press
60 Shipview Lane
Sequim, WA 98382
Telephone: 917-428-8312
Email: headmistresspress@gmail.com
Website: headmistresspress.blogspot.com

I have had many teachers, many star-bright and beautiful supporters—family and friends—on this journey with me, and, to all of them, such love and thanks. This book is for Eve and Madeline, with all my heart. For Jane, who listened when there were no words. For Anna Marie Rouse, always.

# Contents

## I. *Acid*

| | |
|---|---|
| Coatlicue Frida and Thorns | 1 |
| The Accident | 2 |
| What Frida Said | 3 |
| Ascension | 5 |
| Avaritia | 6 |
| Tell Me | 7 |
| The Answer | 8 |
| Abjection | 9 |
| The Heroine of Pain | 10 |
| The Accident II | 11 |
| Audience | 12 |
| Love's Anatomy | 13 |
| Acid and Tender | 14 |
| The Answer II | 15 |
| Frida to Her Hummingbird | 16 |

## II. *Tender*

| | |
|---|---|
| In the house of birds | 19 |
| Voyeur | 20 |
| What She Wants to Tell You | 21 |
| Children of Nod | 22 |
| Meet Me in the Supernova | 23 |
| When Marie Antoinette Comes to Wish You a Happy Birthday | 24 |
| Chiromancer | 25 |
| Goddess of the Cornfield | 26 |
| Blue Riding Hood | 28 |
| Phoenix in a Coffee Shop | 29 |
| Josephine | 30 |
| Letter to Little Hummingbird | 31 |
| *About the Author* | 33 |
| *Acknowledgments* | 35 |

*Acid*

## Coatlicue Frida and Thorns

She sculpts a shawl of thorns
and no one speaks
of the slow rolling blood rivulets
caressing her neck.

Because you see determined
Because you see calm
Because she commands the room
and crowns herself with monarchs

don't assume *

*she resurrects herself each morning
at the sacrificial stone. *she sleeps with anyone—
her fucking has never been your business and
for too long. *she is tragic. *she is catastrophic. *she is
outside the bounds of simple caring.

Must we ignore the fullness of possibility?
Hummingbird of sun or war? Are you force
and conquest? Is she severed
or mending? Your country is not
her country. In her house there is always
another beginning. Around her neck
she has unwoven your Christ. You think she
might've loved you only. Listen,
someone else will come.

# The Accident

You know, it is something
to wake in clouds of gold
and blood, to look down
at a body that once
was your own. To feel
like you've left. Only
to return again in pieces.

# What Frida Said

When you are
the ex-voto,
wax and blood
and burning,
cheek to cheek
with a saint,
and you offer
the bread,
the body,
the being,
the brain,
don't tell me
you don't
somehow want to
be saved,
that there is
no expectation
in the giving.

You would rest
your fingers against
my broken pelvis.
You would ask
for tequila-soaked
kisses. You would
take my story
as your story,
and it would never
be your story.

If you paint
and paint again
from what is broken,
which pieces will you
always put back?

And when god comes for you
and asks were you brave
or were you a coward,
will you have loved,
opened and always?
What will you tell her?

# Ascension

Bits of sinew and
silver. Blood thick
and orbit.
        lost galaxies between your legs
Turn yourself mermaid.
        shut this shit down
Set the ground
on fire. Wear a ball gown
of flame. Corset the rib-
cracking cries and
strap on your final
pair of wings. Erase
desire in all its graceless
splendor. What
has it shown you
anyway?

# Avaritia

I pace the hall near your door
until I am certain
you have not left me.

Sunflower to the light,
this soul and its
listlessness.

You are stern.
You are unforgiving.
You say, *ask for
what you need.*

(And the silence
spines and pools
like blood. This virgin
plate. This cactus fruit.)

You say, *stop painting
the marigolds.*
You say, *you will
never hold me
in art.*

Let me tell you
how I need you
near me.
Let me say, *I paint
the flowers so they
will not die.*

## Tell Me

How many times will you paint
a birth only to realize
all you will ever hold is a brush,
a tube of phthalo blue,
veins like ribbons strung
through your spoken fingers,
your own head sprouting
through thorns, your feet into
melons, Mexico, rooting
you. Or to you. Mexico?

How many times will you insist
on the moment of conception
as betrayal. And the women
against your lips as endless
losses? Adoration
is a disease you cling to,
vines feeding from
everything you touch.
Or take. You are.
Taken. How much
have you taken? Even
though you insist
we all thrive on
this one body,
broken. I look
for you
every
where. I deserve
your answer.

# The Answer

*Aren't you betrayed, Querida? Pobrecita. That is art. That is life. Country. Home. Are you welcomed and admired? Sometimes. Are you cursed and called a crazy whore? Maybe—if you're lucky enough to be such a powerful, threatening woman. Are you a child thrown from a bus? Always.*

# Abjection

In the abject there is no balance.
No meditative state.
No drift or float.
When you make your pain your art your pain your art your pain
        your art your pain,
what hangs in the liminal space?
And who will be with you there—if
you aren't a being—
and you
transcend the need
to belong?

They will want to give you clean sheets.
They will want to cauterize
those veins and return
your uterus to its
proper place.
That's what they do.
They will want to medicate you
and
pat your arm.
And they will feel grateful
in the middle of
all that waste,
all that taboo
and exhibit;
they will feel giddy
because the gift
you have given them
is that they are
not you.

# The Heroine of Pain

Make me of flames
and sugar. Take
a vein between
your teeth and pretend
we are somehow
tethered. Tie off
and sink your
needle deep.         I will never
turn away
the way
your eyes demand
I see you:
in violence
in love
in the flowers
at your feet.

They will tell you
that in the final frantic
heat of it all,
my skeleton head
reared itself
and grinned.

O how you need me.
You need me.

# The Accident II

Art is selfish and unkind.
It might change the shape
of your suffering—or someone else's
for a few moments.　　　　Distraction.　　Noise.

But there is no sound
like a dead child
being torn from your body.
Then you know
what is and isn't
about you.

# Audience

I was never certain
who I was supposed
to be here. And so I brought
you to my suffering.
It was effective,
if ill-advised. And, god knows,
I chose ill advisors. How often
do you catch yourself thinking,
why would she live like that?
Only to realize you live like that.
There might be parrots or
packs of hairless dogs
at your feet. You might paint
the ugly monkey on your
back or call her so drunk
and sweet from a bar down
the street. Just to sleep
in someone's arms again.
You have long been too old
for such things. But passion
breeds a kind of reckless
offspring and whisper. Oranges
and sea spray in her hair.
I would have taken you
anywhere. Sometimes
we are all accident and
kiss. Sometimes we
are carnage and rain.

## Love's Anatomy

Here is the window—
your breath and back against,
my hand on the glass and longing,
tethered tethered.
There was nothing surreal in our self-portrait
of stars. Fallen. Flooded and spilled
this womb through all our fingers.
I tried so hard to catch you—
stitched and severed—but when I opened
my mouth to scream, only my heart flew out.
A child's balloon. A lost umbilicus.

I will have to walk out of here alone.
I will have to change my name.
Once more I will have to love
something that I will lose.

Tell me again the story of why we are here.
Tell me again the story of hummingbirds and thorns.

## Acid and Tender

You stand on pedestals,
upstage, hovering in shadow.
You wait for me to pull
you into the light. Don't you
know: I want you
to choose the self
you want me to see.

One of you is in a suit
too large and suspendered
and silly. Your grin.
One of you is all thorns
and stoicism, not a breath
of air between us. And one
of you is shedding
all your organs, trading
for wings. Scalpel
and spine. You pull
your rib cage apart. You
feed me small bits
of your petrified heart.
I will never know
who we were
supposed to be.

# The Answer II

Apologies
are just lies
and offerings.

For the feelings
we never allow
ourselves to live.

# Frida to Her Hummingbird

This bird at my throat,
exotic and dead, webbed
in thorns. If her feathers
fall like petals of sun,
I might catch one
and begin to build
the cloak of a goddess.

I might ask for too much.
But I no longer believe
that love is illness. Or
that you should be far
from me. Stay still at my
breast, tiny warrior.
Wings of fire and
returned spirits. Desire
and display thread
themselves, a nest.
We must protect
each other, Querida,
my soft soul
mate.

Here, help
disguise me, in
a song of iridescence,
and I will bring us
the moon.

*Tender*

## In the house of birds

walls quiver with wings.
Her nervous fingers
flutter at her ruby
throat. And every room
has a pedestaled bath,
where delicate finches
dip tiny beaks while
regal hawks hang
from birch chandeliers.
Why am I here, she wonders
again. Her hollow womb,
her spindly ankles? Oh,
yes, of course,
her head. "Hummingbird,"
they said, when she told
them she craved nectar
and couldn't sit still.
"Sanctuary," they said,
when she stopped sleeping
and plucked the feathers
from her crown. It wasn't
this she expected to be.

Not all birds sing
here, she noted.
Some spend all day
constructing meticulous
nests. Others plumping
elaborate plumage.
"Multiple
personalities," hummed
the pigeon, as he hopped
upon her bed.
"Rest,"
she whispered,
but her legs
never
touched
down.

# Voyeur

And the girl
with the hummingbird head,
well, she was lovely
as a nun, so draped and scaled
and dragon-fiery.
She watched everything
so carefully—
the way the husband and wife
shared a fish in emerald
green. Each bite
caught
in the other's teeth. She thought
it might be romantic
to love a fish so much
and knives and forks.
He was a fork for sure,
pointy and bow-tined. The wife
looked lovely in lemon,
like honey and sun,
running through the hummingbird's
fingers. Wingless. Knife.
Wife. Take
the scarlet heart
and her lips. She turns
her head so quickly
and swears they have
this dinner every night.

# What She Wants to Tell You

*There are three things that might save you—*
her voice in smoky alto whisper,
her arms stretched, a jurassic wing span,
in a flicker flight of lightning—
*and there are three things that won't.*
(Insert here a strain of sinister laughter
or three kisses on the top of your head.)
Now make your way home.
I sit on a weeping hill in the rain.  I sit beside a sick bed in complete silence.
I look out onto the orchard.  I gather all my strength like apples in a bucket.
This bucket has a small hole, imperceptible        and the apples look serene
to anyone who passes.  A soul slips through
like liquid silver.         I cup the liquid in thick fingers tight
hand
under
hand.                             Each time something else evaporates
I'm guessing at least one of the three things
I need to show you
is gone.
There is silver all over my hands and I am opening them to show how hard I'm trying.
And when I do this, when I would
announce I have the answer,
my mouth, so desirous,
so eager, is flooded
with
apples.

# Children of Nod

She took them from a cloud,
resting lazily in the grass. *Just taking a break
from being so high,* the cloud
grinned back, looking slightly
like the Cheshire cat. *Of course you want them,*
he said, *these three tiny children to tend,
but mind the crocodiles as you pass and the sleeping
scorpions. You might lose them again.
And this hasn't been so storybook for you,
has it?* She lurched forward with her arms
of bundles. Her face like worried stone.
Why must she always be so careful? Setting
each one gently down in the striped house,
she dared to catch a breath as they slept
in softness. When midnight came and the sash
split again, she screamed, as white roses spilled
from her mouth. And empty hands.

# Meet Me in the Supernova

I wonder about Easter starfish and rabbits
with rainbow eyes that explode into chalk
when the should've-been-plump twins
giggle madly.　　I wanted you madly once
with a hummingbird kind of frenzy.
And then I turned my back
on the audience.　　　The twins draw
knives and cabbages.

benzos make my mouth turn slack and awe-less.　　　Like that.
Like a giant Q,
full-mouthed O and comet. Hold tight to
the tail. I will come for
you.

If an arm falls off an Easter starfish
will it grow back and walk
on water? Four tiny hands
covered in chalk. Maybe now they
talk to rabbit god and collapse
rainbows in their fists. I think
I loved them madly,
these small kings.

Now I wait for blow darts and stars
from the galaxies where
things are fine, not lost, without me.
I imagine they float in curls
of nautilus shells, that one day
they will send a note.

# When Marie Antoinette Comes to Wish You a Happy Birthday

And then she said,
"Let them eat space!"
Because it was all spinning
wildly by this point
like shiny blue macarons—
the French kind, of course.
And after a few Manhattans,
she hiccoughed, "I do
love a good pied,
don't you?" We couldn't say no,
so we spun one nice and
slow on the record
player.

What a towering head of cake!
We licked all the icing from
her brow and pointy
party hat. She laughed
her smoker's laugh
and called us cannibals.
Her tiny tin skirt
turned to a cone filled
with ice and syrup,
and we all fell in.

But, no matter what,
she was a true satellite—you
had to admit. One of those
days you'll never forget,
as she kicked her spiked heels
into the punch and
called me Judy. I have to say
I never had the urge
to kiss her, but when she
left our orbit,
a balloon popped.

# Chiromancer

This is the line where I push you away—
see how it breaks and breaks again;
Root of the middle finger, Mount of Saturn.
Wisdom in abundance

or rings full and taciturn?
By now in the reading
I have usually tried
to destroy us at least once.
That double-lined Girdle
of Venus, denoting lust.

Instead, tonight, let
the line of the moon ascend.
Let me linger in your
lace-work skin. Sit beside me,
take my hand.

## Goddess of the Cornfield

She says in a voice
reminiscent of the rapture:
"It will all happen again,
with or without you."

The new sky emerges
from an open fist of spring.
A statue here in a winter-
torn field, all thigh and calf
planted, she waits
for the dust to stop
its frenzied dance
around her. She is holding
the light, fierce in her belly.
She carries the clouds,
full of bloom, in her wide-
open fingers. Hear the subtle
crack in her smile, slow
to thunder and watercolor
rage. She is all emerging,
golden. She is all falling,
plum-gray crocus. She pretends
at night she doesn't remember
the winter when
she went away. The winter
when you took the light
and turned her under. Thunder
of soil raining
on a grave.

And maybe that is what
it took to wake
her. How the words
*brave* and *shame*
split

the last
breath
of air
between
them
and sputtered,
"choose."

# Blue Riding Hood

Eventually the wolf
was her grief and she
kept opening the door
to find fierce and ominous
teeth in her grandmother's
clothing. Other days,
six coyotes circled
her in the woods—
her blue cloak and graying
temples. Her hands kept
shaking. She tried to be
still. She lit
signal fires and howled
at merciless stars.        What
big eyes you have, all twelve
of them. And why do they
snarl?        She decided
to name the chupacabras
and pack them gently in her
pickup. She realized
everyone was out to get them
and weren't they just
doing their best to be
magical beasts,
to heal themselves,
to remain
a mystery?

## Phoenix in a Coffee Shop

In the beginning, there is another
beginning. I will bring no one
you know. I will bring nothing you
remember. No one packed
my things. But it doesn't really
matter. Do you see how the edges
blur—old lumber and patinaed metal,
idle hands raising cups, lowering
cups, and mouths that no longer
listen? I will bring
an odd kind of laughter,
slopping against the sides
of this wide-open
wound. Coffee black, no
sugar. In the beginning,
I let you.

In the beginning, the beginning asks
that I bring another. I will expect
no one. I will not ask for
permission. I have risen
from the middle so many times,
even the ashes are uncertain.
I will part the room
in a sea of red. I will
reassure. Pat your hand.

In the beginning,
the beginning makes it clear.
There is nothing
left of what I knew.

# Josephine

Not like keys or reading glasses
Not like photos decaying in a box     Not like
the doll I named
my name. No.
Here are the ways I chime
your name on a rainbow
xylophone. A chorus
of the never forgottens,
how this lotus womb heaved
you to the heavens. And so
I must require that your
great and grand mothers sing
to you in silver dresses
the lullabies I was not allowed.
And sometimes a silly clown
juggles over the clouds just so
a soft and perfect giggle
launches my heart to where
the stars turn to Xs, marking
every spot where I might (but will never)
find you again.

## Letter to Little Hummingbird

Her grandmother of the
ruby throat and tiny slippers,
of the summer fly swatters
and iced tea in thin
snifters —she taught her
the magic of moveable beasts:

*Dear Hummingbird Girl,*
              *Nowhere is always near*
*and you command*
*the air, my dear.*
She laughed in pale pinks
and swore in pirate sonnets.

*This is your cake and*
*the winking typewriter.    Mind the Ps,*
*they stick like Qs,*
*the sonsabitches,    but they*
*will do well by you.*

*And as for your head,*
*when it passes to you,*
*it will hold the scent*
*of Shalimar and*
*all my secrets.*
*Like how to cheat*
*at crosswords and*
*reassemble your sanity*
*with sugar cubes*
*and the gentle hand of a good woman.*
*Let her lead you.*

*Each sequin is a song*
*and mind your speed*
*on icy nights. And never let*
*your head fly off. Make each*
*choice yourself, and, remember,*
*I was made to love you.*

## About the Author

Jen Rouse works as a consulting librarian at Cornell College in Mount Vernon, IA. She is a poet and playwright. Her play, *For the Care and Control of the Insane,* was published by *Masque & Spectacle* and performed in the Underground New Play Festival at Theatre Cedar Rapids. Another play, *Conjure,* was directed by the most amazing Janeve West and produced by SPT Theatre Co. Her deepest delight, however, is every moment spent with her brilliant daughter Madeline.

# Acknowledgments

My thanks to the editors of the following publications, in which these poems first appeared:

*Hot Tin Roof:* "In the house of birds"

*MadHat Lit:* "Letter to Little Hummingbird"

*MadHat Lit:* "What She Wants to Tell You"

*Pretty Owl Poetry:* "When Marie Antoinette Comes to Wish You a Happy Birthday"

# Headmistress Press Books

*Lovely* - Lesléa Newman
*Teeth & Teeth* - Robin Reagler
*How Distant the City* - Freesia McKee
*Shopgirls* - Marissa Higgins
*Riddle* - Diane Fortney
*When She Woke She Was an Open Field* - Hilary Brown
*God With Us* - Amy Lauren
*A Crown of Violets* - Renée Vivien tr. Samantha Pious
*Fireworks in the Graveyard* - Joy Ladin
*Social Dance* - Carolyn Boll
*The Force of Gratitude* - Janice Gould
*Spine* - Sarah Caulfield
*Diatribe from the Library* - Farrell Greenwald Brenner
*Blind Girl Grunt* - Constance Merritt
*Acid and Tender* - Jen Rouse
*Beautiful Machinery* - Wendy DeGroat
*Odd Mercy* - Gail Thomas
*The Great Scissor Hunt* - Jessica K. Hylton
*A Bracelet of Honeybees* - Lynn Strongin
*Whirlwind @ Lesbos* - Risa Denenberg
*The Body's Alphabet* - Ann Tweedy
*First name Barbie last name Doll* - Maureen Bocka
*Heaven to Me* - Abe Louise Young
*Sticky* - Carter Steinmann
*Tiger Laughs When You Push* - Ruth Lehrer
*Night Ringing* - Laura Foley
*Paper Cranes* - Dinah Dietrich
*On Loving a Saudi Girl* - Carina Yun
*The Burn Poems* - Lynn Strongin
*I Carry My Mother* - Lesléa Newman
*Distant Music* - Joan Annsfire
*The Awful Suicidal Swans* - Flower Conroy
*Joy Street* - Laura Foley
*Chiaroscuro Kisses* - G.L. Morrison
*The Lillian Trilogy* - Mary Meriam
*Lady of the Moon* - Amy Lowell, Lillian Faderman, Mary Meriam
*Irresistible Sonnets* - ed. Mary Meriam
*Lavender Review* - ed. Mary Meriam

www.ingramcontent.com/pod-product-compliance
Lightning Source LLC
Chambersburg PA
CBHW070040070426
42449CB00012BA/3110